How To
WRITE A
RESEARCH
PAPER
STEP BY STEP

by **PHYLLIS CASH**

HERBERT H. LEHMAN COLLEGE

MONARCH PRESS

First Printing: 1983
Copyright © 1977 by
Phyllis Cash

Published by
MONARCH PRESS
A Simon & Schuster Division of
Gulf & Western Corporation
Simon & Schuster Building
1230 Avenue of the Americas
New York, N.Y. 10020

MONARCH PRESS and colophon are trademarks of
Simon & Schuster, registered in the U.S. Patent and
Trademark Office.

Standard Book Number: 0-671-47093-0

10 9 8 7 6 5 4

Printed in the United States of America

Dedication

This book is dedicated to the
most important men in my world;
Mark, Steve, David, and Syd

Acknowledgments

For permission to excerpt and reprint material in this book, the author and publisher are grateful to the following:

Lehman College
for the use of the library facilities and assistance of their librarians.

Simon and Schuster
for excerpts from *The Psychology of Achievement*, by Walter B. Pitkin. Copyright © 1930 by Walter B. Pitkin.

for excerpt from *After Conviction*, by Ronald L. Goldfarb and Linda R. Singer. Copyright © 1973 by Ronald L. Goldfarb and Linda R. Singer.

for excerpt from *Political Handbook & Atlas of the World, 1968*, by Walter H. Mallory, ed. Copyright © 1968 by The Council on Foreign Relations.

Salvatore L. Scorzello for the research paper "The Condition of the American Indians."

The H. W. Wilson Company
for material from the *Readers' Guide to Periodical Literature*. Reprinted by permission of the publisher, The H. W. Wilson Company.

CONTENTS

INTRODUCTION

A term paper—often called a research paper—is a work which gives the results of the writer's investigation of a particular topic. Although an occasional research paper may be based wholly or partially on interviews and personal observation, the great majority of such investigations are carried out in a library, where the writer gathers facts and expert opinions from books, periodicals, and other sources.

Although the research paper is based on the ideas and work of others, you should not think of it as a mechanical process. In summarizing and relating facts and ideas from several sources, you will have plenty of chance to use your creativity and to show the kind of thinking which you are capable of. You will also, of course, be demonstrating your ability to express your ideas effectively and gracefully.

Over the years a standard procedure for doing a research paper has evolved. This book is a step-by-step guide to this standard procedure. Both the procedure and this book are divided into three parts: the first part (Steps 2–5) is concerned with finding an appropriate subject; the second (Steps 6–10) deals with the research process; the third (Steps 11–16) gives help in writing the paper. When you have completed all these steps, you will have a finished paper ready to hand in.

Most of the steps in this book are divided into three sections: Presentation, Recognition, and Application. The Presentation sections give information and principles that you will need to complete a particular step. The Recognition sections contain exercises that will give you a chance to practice what you have learned. Answers to these exercises are given in Appendix A. Each of the Application sections gives detailed guidance in applying what you have learned to the term paper that you are writing as you work through this book. Some of the steps have only one or two of these sections.

UNIT ONE — DEVELOPING THE SUBJECT

When instructors assign research papers, they usually mention a fairly broad subject within which students are expected to find their own topics. For example, an instructor in an American literature course might ask for a paper on any author studied in the course. A music teacher may require a paper on any phase of twentieth-century music. A history professor may ask students to investigate any aspect of the American labor movement. In each of these cases it is the student's job to develop a specific topic which can be adequately treated in the length of paper which has been asked for.

The steps in this unit are concerned with how you go about selecting a specific subject, how you decide what organizational pattern will be most appropriate, and how you develop a thesis statement, that is, a brief statement of what you intend to do in your paper. These initial steps are designed to provide a focus for your research. Therefore they should be completed before you go to the library.

At the same time, however, you should also look upon these early decisions as tentative. As you do research and get deeper into your subject, you are likely to look at things differently, and this may well lead to adjustments in your topic, in your chosen pattern of organization, or in your thesis statement. You should not regard such changes in course as setbacks. They are, rather, signs that you are doing some good thinking and are getting nearer to your goal.

1

Step 1 — Getting Started

Each paper has basic requirements which you should take into account right from the beginning:

1. Date due: As assigned by your instructor. The recommended schedule for doing the steps in this book takes from seven to nine weeks (see the breakdown with the Contents). This will allow you to proceed carefully and also give adequate time for any necessary reconsiderations or revisions.

2. Length: As assigned. A *page* usually means double-spaced typing on 8½-by-11-inch paper. Such a page contains about 250 words.

3. Footnotes: Your footnotes should follow the form given in the Documentation section in Appendix B. Place them at the bottom of the page unless your instructor prefers another position.

4. Bibliography: A listing of the sources you have used is placed at the end of the paper. The bibliography should follow the form given in the Documentation section.

5. Cover sheet: You should provide an initial page which includes the title of the paper, the name of the course for which it has been written, the instructor's name, your name, and the date.

Appendix C contains a detailed Self-Evaluation Guide which you will be using to check your completed paper. You will find it helpful to read it over now to get an idea of the standards that you will have to meet.

In addition to this book you will need the following to complete your paper:

1. Two sizes of ruled index cards, 3-by-5-inch for listing sources and 4-by-6-inch for taking notes.

2. A dictionary for checking spelling, syllabication, meaning, etc.

3. A thesaurus or book of synonyms for helping you use a variety of words in your writing.

Step 2 — Choosing a Topic

Your first task is to take the assignment as given by your instructor and develop for yourself an appropriate topic. In order to do this it helps to know what the characteristics of a good topic are as well as some of the main ways that a topic can be defective.

Presentation

A research paper is expected to be a detailed examination of a particular topic; it is also expected to be based on a variety of sources. A topic is too broad if a much longer paper than you are to write would be required to treat it in a detailed fashion. A topic is too narrow if a sufficient variety of sources cannot be found with which to work. Whether a topic is too narrow depends therefore to some extent on the resources of the library that you plan to use for your research. A topic is too personal if it relies heavily on your own feelings, experiences, opinions. A topic is too technical if the research requires specialized knowledge that you are unable to provide.

In the table on page 4 are some topics that have been developed from five different subjects. Study them and try to decide why they are labeled (1) too broad, (2) inappropriate, or (3) good to start with.

Subject	Too Broad	Sample Topics Inappropriate	Good to Start With
20th-century music	popular music	why I like the Beatles (too personal)	imagery in the Beatles' songs
19th-century military history	the West and the Indians	my opinion of Sitting Bull (too personal)	Sitting Bull and Custer's Last Stand
the American labor movement	unionism in America	organizing a union local (too technical)	how the paraprofessionals working for the New York City Board of Education became part of the United Federation of Teachers
the history of ethnic groups in the United States	the history of the Puerto Ricans	one reason for Puerto Rican migration to the mainland (too narrow)	an analysis of Puerto Rican migration to the mainland in the 1940's
any author studied in your American literature course	Emerson as a famous American writer	Emerson as a child (too narrow)	Hindu philosophy and Emerson

Recognition

Listed below are ten possible topics for a research paper. Next to each topic put a *B* if you think it is too broad, an *I* if you think it is inappropriate, or a *G* if you think it would be a good topic to start with.

___1. the procedure for kidney transplants

___2. kinship among the Bantu

___3. exercise and the prevention of heart disease

___4. how Billie Holiday died

___5. Marcus Garvey's role in the "Back to Africa" movement

___6. the history of Africa

___7. a comparison of Billy Budd and Moby Dick as symbols of virtue

___8. why I want to go to college

___9. the development of American law

__10. some recent trends in drug abuse among high school students

The answers are given in Appendix A. If you got any of the answers wrong, study the examples given in the Presentation again.

Application

Now you are ready to develop your own topic. The following step-by-step procedure will show you how to do it.

Objective: To choose a topic which will be suitable for the paper you have been asked to write.

Procedure:

1. List all of the topics you can think of that fall within the assigned area.

_____

_____

_____

2. When you have spent a few minutes thinking of topics, go back over your list marking each topic with a *B* if it is too broad, an *I* if it is inappropriate, or a *G* if it would be a good starting topic.

3. Now consider the topics marked *G* and decide which one you would most like to work with.

4. If you are not satisfied with the topic you have come up with, wait a day or two and repeat the procedure. Remember that you will be spending several weeks with your topic, so if at all possible it should be something that you have a real interest in working on.

Step 3 — Matching the Topic with Organizational Patterns

Once you have decided on your topic, it is important to begin thinking about how you can develop it. One of the best ways to proceed is to consider different organizational patterns and decide which one or which ones would be appropriate for your topic.

Presentation

Here are the five most common organizational patterns:

1. Chronological: This pattern treats a topic according to its time sequence. *Example*: Using the topic an analysis of Puerto Rican migration to the mainland in the 1940's, you might concentrate on the years 1940, 1943, 1946, and 1949. You could then point out and explain the trends in Puerto Rican migration which developed during the decade.

2. Comparison-Contrast: This pattern takes two or more aspects of a topic and shows how they are similar and how they differ. *Example*: Using the topic Hindu philosophy and Emerson, you might discuss the characteristics of Hindu philosophy and then

show the ways in which Emerson's work is similar and the ways in which it is different.

3. Topical: This pattern breaks a topic into smaller units, or subtopics, and analyzes each one. *Example*: Using the topic imagery in the Beatles' songs, you might discuss and analyze the symbolism related to such subtopics as drugs and sexual mores.

4. Problem-Solution: This pattern states a problem and then analyzes the solutions proposed by experts in the field. The student may even develop his own solution if he can support it with the research he has done. *Example*: Using the topic how the paraprofessionals working for the New York City Board of Education became part of the United Federation of Teachers, you could discuss the problems the paraprofessionals faced as nonunion members, the problems involved in joining an established union, and the solutions found to these problems by the groups and experts involved.

5. Opinion-Reason: This pattern allows the student to state his opinion about his topic and show how the reasons for this opinion are well supported by the research he has done. *Example*: Using the topic Sitting Bull and Custer's Last Stand, you could express the opinion that a myth has developed which unjustifiably pictures Sitting Bull as a villain and Custer as a hero. Your reasons for this opinion would be shown by your analysis of the myths and historical information about this famous battle.

You may use one organizational pattern or a combination. In fact, it is common to find that two or more organizational patterns are naturally related to a topic. *Example*: Using the topic an analysis of Puerto Rican migration to the mainland in the 1940's, you could use a chronological pattern as suggested above. Then within each time period you could treat as subtopics (topical organization) the various factors which led to migration, such as economic, political, and social factors. Finally, you could give reasons for your opinion as to which of these factors was most important (opinion-reason).

Recognition

Match the topic in column A below with the most appropriate organizational pattern in column B. Be able to tell why you chose your answer. The answers are given in Appendix A.

A	B
1. J. S. Bach was the greatest musician of all time	a. chronological
2. Discrimination in the U.S. Army changed from 1900 to 1946	b. compare/ contrast
3. There are many ways our welfare system can be improved	c. topical
4. Some customs of the Mayan Indians	d. problem-solution
5. Susan B. Anthony and Eleanor Roosevelt as examples of liberated women	e. opinion-reason

For three of the topics above state how you could use a combination of organizational patterns. Compare your answers with the examples given in the Presentation.

_____

_____

_____

Application

Now you are ready to choose organizational patterns for your own paper. Follow the procedure outlined below.

Objective: To choose patterns of organization that might be used in developing your topic.

Procedure:

1. Write down your topic from Step 2.

_____

2. Write the patterns (one or a combination) that you could use for development.

_____

_____

3. In a few sentences combine 1 and 2 and show *how* you will use the patterns to develop your topic.

_____

_____

_____

Step 4 — Preparing an Idea Sheet

Application

At this point you have a starting topic and an idea of the patterns of organization you could use to develop it. You must explore this topic in more depth before you can begin your research. One way to do this is to prepare an idea sheet. The following procedure will show you how to do this.

Objective: To develop an idea sheet that will further refine your starting topic.

Procedure:

1. Do some general reading on your topic, keeping in mind which organizational patterns you have decided will be most promising. This preliminary survey should include the following: (a) a general encyclo-pedia article, and (b) any information you already have, such as class notes, textbooks, and other assigned readings.

2. List all ideas, questions, and reactions that come to mind during this preliminary survey. This idea sheet will help you later in structuring your research. While you are preparing it you may find that your topic is changing and becoming more definite and limited. You may also see new possibilities for using different organizational patterns. You may even find you have so many ideas that you need several pages. All this is progress!

Step 5 — Formulating a Thesis Statement

Once you have chosen a topic, thought about the organizational patterns you might use, and prepared an idea sheet, you are ready for the next important step—formulating a thesis statement. A thesis statement consists of one or two sentences which express what you plan to do with your topic; it is a statement of the aim, the goal, the main idea, of your paper. It should contain an idea that can be developed through scholarly research and which can serve as a tool for maintaining the unity of your paper. All sections of your paper and all the research you use must be related to your thesis statement. As your work on the paper progresses, your topic, organizational patterns, and thesis statement should become closely intertwined. Together they will provide a firm basis for your research.

Presentation

In the table on pages 11-12 are examples of good thesis statements based on the same topics and organizational patterns presented in Steps 2 and 3.

Topic	Organizational Patterns	Thesis Statement
imagery in the Beatles' songs	Topical—discuss the imagery involving sex and drugs and Chronological—use the earliest songs first	The lyrics of the Beatles' songs use a great deal of imagery. Much of this reflects the mores of our culture involving sex and drugs.
Sitting Bull and Custer's Last Stand	Comparison-contrast—show the difference between the myths and the historic realities of Custer's Last Stand	There is a discrepancy between the myth and the reality of Sitting Bull's participation in the battle called Custer's Last Stand. The myth falsely depicts Sitting Bull as a villain and Custer as a hero.
how the paraprofessionals working for the New York City Board of Education became part of the United Federation of Teachers	Problem-solution—show how this group solved the problems of joining an established union and Chronological—trace this movement historically from beginning to end	The paraprofessionals working for the New York City Board of Education are a recent example of workers who were able to join an established, recognized union.

Topic	Organizational Patterns	Thesis Statement
an analysis of Puerto Rican migration to the mainland in the 1940's	Opinion-reason—identify the factors that led to this migration and explain how your research proves they were important and Topical—treat each of the factors under logical subtopics and Chronological—organize these factors in the order in which they developed historically	The Puerto Rican migration to the mainland in the 1940's was caused by several factors.
Hindu philosophy and Emerson	Topical—analyze the aspects of Hindu philosophy which appear in Emerson's writings and Comparison-contrast—show the similarities in Emerson's writings and Hindu literature	Emerson, in his poetry and essays, shows the influence of Hindu philosophy and literature.

The preceding thesis statements are good because:

1. They consist of one or two complete sentences.

2. They state the definite topic of the paper.

3. They give an idea of the approach the writer will take.

4. They are closely related to the set of organizational patterns which are to be used.

5. They can be developed by using sources of expert information—in other words, by research.

Recognition

Put a *T* next to the sentences below that would make good thesis statements. Put an *N* next to those that would not make good thesis statements. Be able to explain why you chose *T* or *N* for each statement. The answers are in Appendix A.

___1. The origin of baseball.

___2. Baseball has its beginnings in several games of ancient times.

___3. President Polk's role in the Mexican War of 1848 reflects his commitment to the policy of Manifest Destiny.

___4. Any society copes with its environment.

___5. The Bantu cope with their environment through the use of their technology, their economic system, and their social groupings.

___6. People behave in peculiar ways.

___7. I find listening to modern jazz extremely relaxing since it helps me forget some of the difficulties of modern life.

___8. The Puritan sense of community of the first generation New Englanders changed to Yankee individualism by the end of the eighteenth century.

___9. The graphic arts can be used to express man's emotions.

___10. The Coleman report had several implications for integrated education on the precollege level.

Application

You are now ready to formulate your own thesis statement for the paper you are writing. Review quickly all the work you have done for your paper so far and all that you have just learned about thesis statements. Then follow the procedure below.

Objective: To formulate a thesis statement for your paper on the basis of your topic, your patterns of organization, and your idea sheet.

Procedure:

1. Study and analyze your idea sheet. Group ideas that seem to be related. Are there any ideas which you find especially interesting?

2. Can you come up with a thesis statement using these ideas? If necessary, reconsider and change your organizational patterns. Then try again to write a thesis statement.

3. Check your thesis statement to be sure that it includes both the topic and what you plan to do with the topic. Your thesis statement should also contain an idea which can be developed by research.

4. Be prepared to repeat 1, 2, and 3. Formulating a thesis statement is challenging, creative work and may take a great deal of trial and error before you are satisfied.

UNIT TWO — FINDING THE MATERIAL

The steps in Unit One were a preparation for research. In Unit Two the scene changes to the library. The steps in this unit will show you how to investigate the resources of your own library, how to find books and articles that are likely to contain useful material, and how to prepare bibliography cards and note cards. When you complete this unit, you should be ready to begin organizing your material and writing your paper.

Step 6 — Exploring the Library

Application

To complete this step you must actually go to the library you plan to use for your research. Answering the questions below will be an efficient way for you to learn how to use it. Following the questions are suggested activities that involve actual use of the library.

Objective: To use questions and activities to learn how to use your library for research.

Procedure:

1. Go to the library and answer the following questions:
    (a) Do you know where each of the following is located? Many libraries have maps posted that will help you.
        (1) card catalogs

      (2) indexes for periodicals, newspapers, and scholarly journals

      (3) volumes of abstracts

      (4) different kinds of books: reference, reserve, circulating, special collections

      (5) periodicals

      (6) audio-visual materials: tapes, cassettes, records, slides, filmstrips, microfilm, microfiche

  (b) Do you know how to use the catalogs, indexes, and abstracts? Do you know where to find books on open shelves? Do you know the procedures for obtaining materials from closed stacks? Can you operate the audio-visual equipment? Have you explored the facilities for making copies?

2. If you answered No to any part of question 1, see the librarian at once for help.

3. Make a floor plan of your library.

4. (a) Find one card in the catalog for each of the following:

      (1) subject card: Hopi Indians

      (2) title card: A History of Art and Music

      (3) author card: Oscar Lewis

  (b) Make out a call slip for each card you found in activity (a).

  (c) List all the information you can find on one of the cards you found in activity (a).

5. (a) Find one entry in the *Readers' Guide to Periodical Literature* for 1970 for each of the following:

      (1) subject: Hallucinogenic drugs

      (2) author: Barbara W. Tuchman

  (b) Make out a call slip for each entry you found in activity (a).

(c) List all the information you can find in one of the entries you found in activity (a).

6. If any of these activities has given you trouble, see the librarian at once for help.

Step 7 — Finding Appropriate Sources

Now you are ready to do independent research for your own topic and thesis. The school library is usually the best place to begin. When you go, be sure to take the following supplies with you:

1. Several pencils for writing bibliography cards and note cards

2. A ballpoint pen for filling out call slips

3. Bibliography cards—3-by-5-inch ruled index cards

4. Note cards—4-by-6-inch ruled index cards (some students use even larger ones)

5. This book; you will especially need the Documentation section in Appendix B as a guide to preparing your cards.

When you get to the library, look up the subject of your paper in the card catalog and in the periodical indexes. If you have trouble finding your subject, ask the librarian for help. Sometimes the catalog system will use a synonym that doesn't occur to you. For example, one student started his research by looking up "Black Americans," and he found nothing. When he asked the librarian, he learned that his subject was listed under "Negro—U.S."

Once you've found your subject, read through the catalog cards and index entries. If any book or article seems as if it might be worthwhile, follow the library's procedure for obtaining it.

Presentation

Below are three sets of topics and thesis statements together with a catalog card and an index entry that seem appropriate for each one. Notice how several parts of the catalog card can be used to decide whether a book will be a good source.

1. Topic: Sitting Bull and Custer's Last Stand

   Thesis: There is a discrepancy between the myth and the reality of Sitting Bull's participation in the battle called Custer's Last Stand. The myth falsely depicts Sitting Bull as a villain and Custer as a hero.

973.82   Custer, George Armstrong, 1839-1876.

           Finerty, John Frederick, 1846–1908.

F 49w   War-path and bivouac; or, The conquest of the Sioux, a narrative of stirring personal experiences and adventures in the Big Horn and Yellowstone Expedition of 1876, and in the campaign on the British border in 1879. With an introd. by Oliver Knight.   Norman, University of Oklahoma Press c. ₍1961₎

        358 p   Illus   20 cm.   (The Western frontier library, 18)

        1. Dakota Indians—Wars, 1876. 2. Nez Percé Indians—Wars, 1877. 3. Custer, George Armstrong, 1839–1876. 4. Crook, George, 1828-1890. 5. Indians of North America—Wars, 1866–1895. I. Title.

E83.866.F52   1961   973.82   61–9001 ‡

Library of Congress   ₍30₎

Floating island: creamy custard desserts: with recipes. E. Alston. il Look 34:64-5 S 22 '70
Oriental switch, savory custards. Sunset 145: 110-11 Ag '70
CUSTER, George Armstrong
   Haunting new vision of the Little Big Horn. il Am Heritage 21:101-3 Je '70
CUSTODIAN accounts. See Custodianship accounts
CUSTODIANSHIP accounts
   Children as tax shelters. Forbes 106:71 N 1 '70
   Put investments in a child's name? il Changing T 24:31-2 F '70

2. Topic: Imagery in the Beatles' songs

 Thesis: The lyrics of the Beatles' songs use a great deal of imagery. Much of this imagery reflects the mores of our culture involving sex and drugs.

ML
3545
.B4
1972

Belz, Carl.
  The story of rock. 2d ed. New York, Oxford University Press. 1972.
    xv. 286 p. ports. 22 cm. $7.50
    "Bibliographical essay": p. 232–243; "selected discography: 1953–1971": p. 244–273.

  1. Music, Popular (Songs, etc.) – History and criticism.
  I. Title

ML3545.B4   1972   784   77–183870
                                                MARC

  Library of Congress   72 [4]   MN

BEATLES
George Harrison tells it like it is; interview; ed. by M. Thomas. G. Harrison. Holiday 43:111-12 + F '68
Inside Beatles, P.D. Zimmerman, pors Newsweek 72:106 + S 30 '68
Log of The yellow submarine. M. Wilk. il McCalls 95:72-5 Ag '68
Mannerist phase; new album of recordings. il Time 92:53 D 6 '68
Polyphony and a new vocal quartet. F.V. Grunfeld. il Horizon 10:56-9 Spr '68

---

3. Topic: Hindu philosophy and Emerson

 Thesis: Emerson, in his poetry and essays, shows the influence of Hindu philosophy and literature.

814   **Emerson, Ralph Waldo,** 1803–1882.

Fm 3ess4   Essays. First series. New York, Clarke, Given & Hooper
ser. 1   ₍n.d.₎

        iv, 326 p. (University edition)
        Binder's title: Emerson's essays, vol. I.

          Contents. – History. Self-reliance. Compensation. Spiritual
      laws. Love. Friendship. Prudence. Heroism. The over-soul.
      Circles. Intellect. Art.

Emerson, Kendall
   Ray of hope in Russia. Outlook 124:74-6 Ja 14 '20
Emerson, Ralph Waldo
   Belaboring the Brahmans again. Lit Digest 63:31 O 4 '19
   Carlyle and Emerson. J. M. Sloan. Liv Age 309:486-9 My 21 '21
   Idol of compensation. M. Moravsky. Nation 108:1004-5 Je 28 '19; Same cond. Cur Opinion 67:179-80 S '19

Recognition

Below are two sets of topics and thesis statements. For each set there are several catalog cards and index entries. Choose the best source from the catalog cards for each set and the best from the index entries. Be prepared to explain briefly the reasons for your choices. Then check the answers in Appendix A.

1. Topic: How the paraprofessionals working for the New York City Board of Education became part of the United Federation of Teachers.

Thesis: The paraprofessionals working for the New York City Board of Education are a recent example of workers who were able to join an established, recognized union.

LB
2844
.1
.A8B7

Brotherson, Mary Lou.
    Teacher aide handbook; a guide for new careers in education ₍by₎ Mary Lou Brotherson ₍and₎ Mary Ann Johnson. Danville, Ill., Interstate Printers & Publishers ₍1971₎

    210 p. Illus., forms. 28 cm.

    Bibliography: p. 163-168.

    1. Teachers' assistants — Handbooks, manuals, etc.   I. Johnson, Mary Ann, 1930-   joint author.   II. Title.

    LB2844.1.A8B7   371.1'412   78-137644
                                                        MARC

    Library of Congress   71 ₍4₎

(a)

L
13
.U483C6

Cole, Stephen, 1941—
    The unionization of teachers; a case study of the UFT. New York, Praeger ₍1969₎

    ix, 245 p. 22 cm. 8.00

    Bibliographical references included in "Notes" (p. 197-215)

    1. **United Federation of Teachers.**   I. Title.

    L13.U483C6   331.881'1'3711   69-15743
                                                        MARC

    Library of Congress   ₍5₎

(b)

LB
2844
.1
.A8W5

Wielgat, Jeanne.
　　An effective teacher-aide program; a detailed presenta-
tion of the place of teacher-aides in the total educational
picture ... Dayton, Ohio, G. A. Pflaum [1969]
　　55 p. Illus., forms. 28 cm. (What's happening) 2.50
　　Based on the teacher-aide program at St. John Chrysostom
School, Bellwood, Ill.
　　Bibliography: p. 53–55.
　　1. Teachers' assistants – Handbooks, manuals, etc.
I St John Chrysostom School, Bellwood, I 11. II. Title.

LB 2844.1. A8W5　　　　371.1'412　　　　71–82523
　　　　　　　　　　　　　　　　　　　　　　　MARC

(c)

TEACHERS aides
　　Aide to learning. K.S. Stone. Engl J 55:124-5
　　　Ja '69
　　Go back to school, your child's school. C. L.
　　　Miller. il McCalls 96:4 Ja '69
　　Organization and training of paraprofessionals.
　　　F. P. Bazeli. bibliog Clear House 44:206-9
　　　D '69
　　Pupil tutors and tutees learn together. J. C.
　　　Fleming. il Today's Ed 58:22-4 O '69; Same
　　　abr. Ed Digest 35:38-40 D '69
　　Reading program with lay aides and programmed
　　　material. C. D. Briscoe. Clear House 43:373-7
　　　F '69

(d)

TEACHERS conferences. See Educational con-
　　ferences
TEACHERS contracts. See Teachers — Contracts
TEACHERS unions
　　Future of collective negotiations. M. Lieber-
　　　man. Educ Digest 37:1-4 F '72
　　Growth of faculty unionization. Sch & Soc
　　　100:82 F '72
TEACHING
　　Classroom and consciousness I, II, III. D. E.
　　　Denton. bibliog Sch & Soc 100:9-11 Ja '72
　　Failure in first-grade. M. M. Harris. Today's
　　　Educ 61:24-5 F '72

(e)

TEACHERS aides
  Newark's parent-powered school; Springfield
  avenue community school. L. Rich. il Am
  Ed 7:35-9 D '71
  Paraprofessionals. il Newsweek 78:47 JL 26 '71
  Theme editor: English teacher's ally. G. F.
  Smith. Clear House 46:116-18 O '71
TEACHERS and students
  After all. J. Sharknas. Today's Ed 60:64 D '71

(f)

2. Topic: An analysis of Puerto Rican migration to the mainland in the 1940's.

Thesis: The Puerto Rican migration to the mainland in the 1940's was caused by several factors.

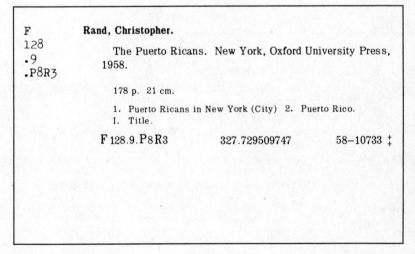

F
128
.9
.P8R3

Rand, Christopher.

    The Puerto Ricans. New York, Oxford University Press, 1958.

    178 p. 21 cm.

    1. Puerto Ricans in New York (City) 2. Puerto Rico.
    I. Title.

    F 128.9.P8R3   327.729509747   58–10733 ‡

(g)

HB
881
P6
1

Puerto Rico   Economic conditions   1918-
Hernández Alvarez, José.
    Return migration to Puerto Rico. Berkeley, Institute of In-
ternational Studies, University of California ₍1967₎

        xiv, 153 p. Illus., maps. 24 cm.   (Population monograph series,
    no. 1)

        Bibliographical footnotes.

        1. Puerto Rico — Emig. & Immig. 2. Puerto Rico — Econ. condit.—
    1918-   I. California. University. Institute of International
    Studies. II. Title. III Series)

    JV7382.H4   325.7295   67–65740

    Library of Congress   ₍3₎

(h)

JV
7381
Z7
E3

Friedlander, Stanley L.
    Labor migration and economic growth: a case study
of Puerto Rico ₍by₎ Stanley L. Friedlander.
Cambridge, Mass., M.I.T. Press ₍1965₎

        ix, 181 p. 24 cm. (M.I.T. monographs in economics)
        Bibliography: p. 173–178.

        1. Puerto Rico — Emig. & Immig. 2. Labor supply—Puerto
    Rico. 3. Puerto Rico — Econ. condit. I. Title. (Series)
    JV7381.Z7E3   331.11097295   65–27233

(i)

PUERTO RICO
Puerto Rico's bootstraps. R. G. Tugwell and
G. F. Tugwell. Harper 194:160-9 F '47
Self-help for Puerto Rico; what is needed in
that distressed island. E. Lonigan. Common-
weal 43:302-5 Ja 4 '46
Solution for Puerto Rico: emigration. Scholastic
48:11 Ap 22 '46
Stricken land: the story of Puerto Rico, by R. G.
Tugwell. S. Welles. Sat R Lit 29:9-11 D 28 '46
What about Puerto Rico? E. S. Jones. Christian
Cent 63:138-40 Ja 30 '46

(j)

PUERTO RICAN students in the United States
See also
Spanish speaking students
PUERTO RICANS in New York City. See Puerto
Ricans in the United States
PUERTO RICANS in the United States
Culture and the people: Museo del bario. R.
Ortiz. Art in Am 59:27 My '71
Puerto Rican migration: right place, wrong time?
N. Glazer. America 125:339-41 O 30 '71
Time to go home. F. Pico. America 126:20-1
Ja 8 '72
PUERTO RICO
See also
Church and social problems — Puerto Rico
Culebra Island
Hotels, taverns, etc. — Puerto Rico
Music festivals — Puerto Rico
Poor — Puerto Rico
San Juan
Tourist trade — Puerto Rico
United Nations — Puerto Rico

(k)

PUERTO RICANS in the United States
Airborne from San Juan. N. Grieser. il New
Repub 117:21-4 N 3 '47
Channel Puerto Rican migration. Commonweal
47:484 F 27 '48
Emigrating Puerto Ricans. Commonweal 46:420
Ag 15 '47
Immigration from the western hemisphere.
K. Davis and C. Senior. bibliog f tabs Ann Am
Acad 262:77-9 Mr '49
Maid problem. New Repub 116:7 Ap 28 '47

(1)

Application

Now you are ready to go to your library to research the
topic and thesis of the paper you are writing.

Objective: To find as many sources of information as are
required for your paper. Be sure to use both books and
periodicals.

Procedure:

1. Using your topic and thesis statement, find books in the card catalog and articles in the indexes which seem appropriate for your paper.

2. Follow your library's procedures for using these materials.

3. You may find at this stage that you must revise or change your topic or thesis because there is too little or too much material. You may also find another, more exciting topic as you are working. Don't hesitate to modify your topic or your thesis; you still have enough time to complete your paper and very little you have done so far will be wasted.

Step 8 — Preparing Bibliography Cards

At this point in your research efforts, you have found materials that seem promising. Before you go on to examine these materials to see what kind of information they provide, you need to know how to make bibliography cards and note cards. The actual preparation of the bibliography— Step 15—is quite a ways off. But you must begin now to handle your sources efficiently if you are to be ready for Step 15.

The bibliography is an alphabetical list of the sources from which you have taken information that you have used in your paper. Each entry in a bibliography must contain certain facts about the source, and these facts must be presented in an acceptable format. Experience has shown that the easiest way to do this is to prepare a bibliography card for each source right at the beginning from which information is taken. The bibliography card should contain all the information that will later be needed in preparing both the bibliography and the footnotes. Should it happen that a source isn't used in the final paper, the card can always be discarded. On the other hand, incomplete or missing bibliography cards can only cause confusion and last-minute rushes to the library.

Sample bibliography cards for the two most common research sources—books and periodicals—are given in the Presentation below. Samples for other kinds of sources can be found in Appendix B.

Presentation

The following information must be included in the bibliography card for a book:

1. author's name, last name first
2. title of the book, underlined
3. where the book was published
4. the publisher's name
5. the year the book was published

This information is usually found on the title page or on the copyright page. It should be arranged on a 3-by-5-inch card like this:

---

author's name   *Cash, Phyllis*

title   <u>*How To Write a Research Paper*</u>

where published   *N.Y.*

publisher   *Simon & Schuster, Inc.*

year published   *1976*

The following information must be included in the bibliography card for a periodical:

1. author's name (of the article itself), last name first
2. title of the article, in quotes
3. name of the periodical, underlined
4. volume number
5. date of the periodical
6. exact pages on which the article appears

This information is usually found on the cover or the masthead page. It should be arranged on a 3-by-5-inch card as follows:

author's name	*Jones, Bill*
title of article	*"The Beatles Are Coming"*
title of periodical	*Modern Music*
volume number	*50*
date of periodical	*June 20, 1965*
exact pages of article	*pgs 5 to 7 and 25 to 30*

Recognition

Here is a list that you can use to check bibliography cards. There are some errors on the sample cards below the list. Next to each error you find put the number of the checklist item which applies. After you complete the exercise, check your answers with the ones in Appendix A.

1. Author's name is on first line.
2. Author's last name is written first.
3. Title of a book is underlined.
4. Place of publication of a book is given.
5. Book publisher's name is given.
6. Year a book was published is given.
7. No page numbers are needed for a book.
8. Title of an article appears in quotes.
9. Name of a periodical is underlined.
10. Volume number of a periodical is given.
11. Date of a periodical is given.
12. Pages on which an article appears are given.

```
Jane Smith

The Life of Sitting Bull



Jarred Publishers

pgs 57-77
```

Doe, John

Life in Puerto Rico

U.S. Digest

pgs. 49-56

Application

This Application should take place at the same time as the Application for Step 10, in which you will be examining the sources you have selected for information that is useful for your paper.

Objective: To write as many bibliography cards as are necessary for the paper you are writing.

Procedure:

1. Each time you find a source you think you may have a use for in your paper, make out a bibliography card.

2. Check to be sure you have included all the information you will need, as shown in Appendix B.

Step 9 — Preparing Note Cards

As you do your research you will need an efficient system for recording the information you find and for keeping track of where it came from. The bibliography card, which was described in Step 8, is one component of such a system; a second component is the note card.

A note card is simply a ruled index card, usually 4 by 6 inches, but sometimes larger, that a researcher uses to record a piece of information that he thinks he may want to use. Such notes can take several forms: (1) a direct quote is a note that you have copied word for word from the source; (2) a paraphrase is a note in which you express another person's ideas in your own words; (3) in an outline note you organize the material in terms of main and subordinate ideas; (4) the summary note is, like the paraphrase, written in your own words, but it is usually longer and covers much more source material. Note cards can also be used for copies of tables, charts, maps, graphs, etc.

Each note card must also include an indication of the source of the material it contains. Usually the author's last name is put at the top center of the card and the page number where the material was found is written in the upper right-hand corner. If you are using two books by the same author, or if the author of a source is not given, you can use part of the title to show where the material came from. It is not necessary to give more complete information about the source because you have already entered that information on a bibliography card. In most cases you will have several note cards from a particular source but only one bibliography card.

In the upper left-hand corner of each note card you should indicate in one or two words the aspect of your topic, or the subtopic, that the material on the card is related to. For example, if you are writing a paper on the history of baseball, you might have subtopics on your cards like "origin," "development," "present form." These subtopics will be very helpful when you organize your material and outline your paper.

Presentation

Following are examples of four different kinds of note cards. Preceding each card is the source material upon which it is based. Notice on each card the subtopic in the upper left-hand corner, the author or title in the center, and the page reference in the upper right-hand corner.

1. Direct Quote Note Card

> **224**   THE PSYCHOLOGY OF ACHIEVEMENT
>
> prodigiously into a ripe old age, never snapping back at the curs that were always yapping at his heels, never uttering an unkind word about foe or rival and never doing an unkind deed. But no more of this. The list is endless. Let him who would scan it further turn to the biographies of the great.
>
> ### The Will to Get Well
>
> The will to live amounts to little unless it is supported by the will to get well. Every physician knows that his hopeless cases are those in which the patient has lost interest in recovering. And his most amazing cures are usually worked upon people who burn with the desire to bounce to their feet

mental factors

Pitkin   224

"The will to live amounts to little unless it is supported by the will to get well. Every physician knows that his hopeless cases are those in which the patient has lost interest in recovering."

2. Paraphrase Note Card

> ### ENERGY 223
>
> accidents, personal misfortunes and similar causes strike down some superior men early in life. Eliminate these from the reckoning, and the connection between high ability and animal energy stands forth.
>
> Among many marks of health, two stand out as the surest and most deeply significant. They are a quick return to equilibrium after a shock and, secondly, high immunity. Both can be noted on the mental levels as well as on the grosser physical planes. And later we shall consider some interesting aspects and specimens. Be it noted in passing that in the intellectual life one of the manifestations of stable equilibrium is swift recovery from harsh criticism, personal rebuffs, financial failure, unpopularity, and similar misfortunes in which one's chosen work is involved. No man of superior ability in writing, in music, in politics, or in science is long withheld from

---

mental factors

Pitkin 223

Two aspects of good health are an ability to bounce back after trauma and a high resistance to such trauma (mental and physical).

3. Outline Note Card

Since the police were paid seventy-five cents for every offender put in jail, they lost money every time Augustus succeeded in having someone released to his custody.

Augustus provided the seeds from which our system of probation has grown. Probation was first formally established in the United States. The system, since emulated by other countries, is considered America's contribution to progressive penology. Today over one half of all convicted offenders in the United States are placed on probation. In 1965 approximately 459,140 adults and 224,948 juveniles were on probation, while 475,042 adults and 123,256 juveniles were in institutions or on parole.[2] Under probation, sentences are suspended and defendants continue to live in their communities under conditions imposed by the court and supervised by probation officers.

Augustus provided probation with its characteristic feature: the personal services of a probation officer (a title that was not applied to Augustus himself but was used by his successors) who views his work with offenders as assistance rather than punishment. He was building, how-

---

Probation in U.S.   Goldfarb   209

I ½ of all convicted offenders on probation

   A 1965: 459,140 adults ⟩ on
          224,948 juveniles ⟩ probation

   B 1965: 475,042 adults ⟩ on
          123,256 juveniles ⟩ probation

4. Summary Note Card

CONGO, DEMOCRATIC REPUBLIC OF THE
(Formerly Belgian Congo)

Capital: Kinshasa
Area: 902,274 square miles
Population: 14,000,000 (1964 estimate)

PRESIDENT

LT. GEN. JOSEPH D. MOBUTU. Assumed power on November 24, 1965, to rule Congo by decree.

PARLIAMENT

A unicameral parliament was established under the new constitution of June 24, 1967. Elections are scheduled to be held early in 1968.

RECENT POLITICAL EVENTS

The Congo obtained its independence from Belgium in 1960, and civil war broke out shortly thereafter. Patrice Lumumba, the first Prime Minister, was assassinated. The most important state, Katanga, seceded and was governed separately by its President Moïse Tshombé. Finally, United Nations troops were called in and after three years of struggle the Central Government in 1963 was able to extend its authority over the whole country. Invited to return to the Congo by leading political figures, Moïse Tshombé did so in June, 1964. In July he was appointed Prime Minister.

On October 15, 1965, President Kasavubu dismissed the Moïse Tshombé government and named Evariste Kimba to form a new administration but his cabinet was not confirmed by Parliament. In the midst of the struggle between Tshombé and Kasavubu, General Joseph D. Mobutu in a bloodless *coup* took over the reins of government and appointed Colonel Léonard Mulamba Prime Minister; but removed him in October 1966 and announced a presidential system of government. He assumed all legislative powers in March 1966.

On April 8, 1967, President Mobutu proposed a new constitution which eliminates all former provincial political structures and provides for a parliament elected every five years and the president elected by popular suffrage every seven years. In a popular referendum held from June 4 to June 14 the new constitution was approved. It became effective June 24, 1967.

On June 30, 1967, former Minister Moïse Tshombé was kidnapped from his refuge in Spain and taken to Algiers where he is imprisoned. On July 5, 1967, a group of mercenary-led dissidents sympathetic to Tshombé revolted against the Mobutu regime and captured the Eastern Congo towns of Bukavu and Kisangani. The rebels abandoned these cities several days later and a group of some 1,000 soldiers from Tshombé's home Province of Katanga and 150 mercenaries led by Jean Schramme regrouped at a plantation near the city of Punia. On August 7 this group returned to Bukavu and captured the town. From September 4 to September 15 a conference of the Organization for African Unity held in Kinshasa passed a resolution offering to evacuate the mercenaries under the auspices of an international organization. In November the mercenaries and Katangese troops crossed the frontier and entered Rwanda.

PARTY PROGRAMS AND LEADERS

Many political parties were formed shortly before independence and many others were formed later. None of the parties were truly national in scope and

Recognition

Below you will find three sample note cards. List the errors you find on each card. Check your answers with the key in Appendix A.

Jones

 Some of the reasons for Puerto Rican migration were economic, political or social. Economic revolved around the wage per hour ratio expected of islanders as future mainlanders.

Drugs in Beatle's lyrics   *25*

 " ..... diamonds is an accepted euphemism for expensive drugs or those crystalline in nature."

Beatle's lyrics

Brill

The Beatles are considered an interesting group to listen to and analyze.

Application

As with the Application for Step 8, this Application should take place at the same time as the Application for Step 10.

Objective: To write as many note cards as you will need for the paper you are writing.

Procedure:

1. Each time you come across information that you think will be useful, prepare a note card. Be sure to use the most appropriate note-taking skill (direct quote, paraphrase, outline, summary). You should use combinations of these skills whenever necessary.

2. Check to be sure you have included the subtopic, the author or title, and the page where you found the information.

Step 10 — Finding Appropriate Information

Application

Now that you've found books and periodicals you think you can use, and now that you know how to prepare bibliography cards and note cards, you are ready to begin examining sources to see if you can locate and extract information that will be useful for your paper. In doing this, follow this procedure of previewing, skimming, and reading.

Objective: To use several sources to find appropriate information for your paper.

Procedure:

1. To find appropriate information in a book
   (a) Look in the table of contents for relevant chapters.
   (b) Look in the index for pages which may contain relevant material.
   (c) Do the appendixes contain information you can use?
   (d) Is there a list of charts, maps, illustrations which may be helpful?
   (e) Once you've located the parts of the book which you can use, follow the suggestions under 2.

2. To find appropriate information in periodical articles
   (a) Read the title, subtitles, and captions of illustrations within the selection.
   (b) Read the entire first paragraph of the selection.
   (c) Read the first line of every paragraph in the selection.
   (d) Read the entire last paragraph of the selection.
   (e) Do the charts, maps, or illustrations contain information you can use?

(f) At any point where you think you've found something worthwhile, *read* that entire section carefully.

3. To take the information from the source

(a) When you've decided to use the book or article,
immediately make out a bibliography card. (See
Step 8.)

(b) Make out a note card whenever you find information you think you can use. (See Step 9.)

4. Remember that any additional sources that you find
in the books or articles you read should be investi-
gated.

5. Now that you are at the heart of the research process
you may find information that will lead you to change
your topic or thesis. Be open-minded and ready to
follow any intellectual trail that seems promising.
Such an attitude will lead to a better paper.

UNIT THREE — WRITING THE PAPER

Now that you have collected all your information, you must begin to think about organizing it and putting it in written form. The steps in this unit deal with outlining, with the problems of writing several drafts, with documentation through footnotes and a bibliography, and with typing and proofreading the final version. By the end of this unit you will have a completed paper ready to hand to your instructor.

Step 11 — Outlining the Paper

The first step in actually writing your paper is to organize your information and ideas. The best way to do this is to make a detailed sentence outline of the entire paper. An outline can be revised easily and serves as the skeleton for your paper. If the outline is done well, the actual writing of the paper becomes much easier.

Before you start the outline, take all your note cards and group them according to the subtopics you have put in the upper left-hand corner. Then take each card and arrange them in the order you think you will use them, rearranging them until they are as well organized as possible. Your note cards enable you to organize your paper by shuffling cards rather than by writing, rewriting, and crossing out.

When your cards have been arranged to your satisfaction, check to see that your topic, thesis, and note cards are unified. If they aren't, don't be afraid to change your topic or thesis to conform with the research you have done. You may also discover a need for additional research. If you have followed the suggested schedule, you still have three weeks in which to complete your work.

Once your note cards are organized, your subtopics become the main ideas in your outline, and your note cards can be used as supporting details and subdetails. As you do your outline, keep your note cards in the order in which they appear in the outline. After you've completed the outline, number your note cards consecutively and place the number of each note card next to the place you will use it in your outline. The outline will take a great deal of time. You may have to revise it many times. However, the better your outline, the easier it will be to write your paper.

Presentation

Outline A is a general form; Outline B is by a student.

Outline A

Your name   Course

Date   Instructor

Title of Your Paper

Thesis: Write your thesis statement here.
Pattern: List the patterns you will use here.

Paragraph 1.
{
Introduction:
  Write your opening sentences here. Be sure to include your thesis statement.

Paragraphs 2., 3., 4., etc.
{
Development:
  I. Main Idea Sentence
    A. Supporting detail sentence
      1. subdetail sentence (if needed; use 2, 3, etc., if needed)
    B. Supporting detail sentence
    C. Supporting detail sentence (use D, E, F, etc., if needed)
  II. Another Main Idea Sentence
    A. Supporting detail sentence (if needed, use supporting details and subdetails as shown above)
  III. Continue with as many paragraphs as you need for all your main ideas.

Final
paragraph { Conclusion:
            Summarize your paper; review the thesis
            statement; give your conclusions.

Outline B

David Stevens   History 78
June 3, 1974   Dr. Syd Marks

Some Sources of Job Discrimination Against
Black Americans

Thesis: The federal government and some large trade
unions have acted so as to perpetuate job discrimination against Black Americans.

Patterns: (a) Topical   (b) Comparison-Contrast

Introduction:

Black Americans have suffered many injustices as a
minority group in this country. One of the most devastat-
ing areas of racial injustice concerns the economic aspects of the Black American's life. Much of this injustice
has been perpetuated by the federal government and
some large trade unions.

I. The federal government has been a passive agent for the
past thirty years.

A. Job equality has been a requirement in government
contracts since 1941, when F.D.R. passed it into law.[1]

1. Penalty for noncompliance is cancellation of the
contract.[2]

2. In thirty years, not one contract has ever been
cancelled.[3]

B. One out of every three jobs is due to government
contracts with private corporations.[4]

II. Trade unions have failed to end job discrimination to the
extent that they could.

A. Existing apprenticeship programs prevent minority
groups from entering certain trades.

B. Certain government sponsored plans have proved in-
effective.
1. "Chicago Plan"[5]
2. "Outreach Program"[6]

Conclusion:
The federal government and large trade unions must
evaluate their role in adding to the burden of the Black
American through economic discrimination. Steps can
then be taken to be sure that all Americans are given
opportunities for economic progress, security, and personal growth.

Note: The raised numbers indicate the use and order of the
student's note cards.

Recognition

Compare Outline C with Outlines A and B. There are ten
errors in Outline C. List these errors and then check your
answers with the answer key in Appendix A.

Outline C

Brian Samuels   English 100
April 20, 1974   Dr. Abram Selig

Introduction:
Ralph Waldo Emerson, in his poetry and essays, shows
the influence of Hindu philosophy and literature.

Development:
I. The four Hindu concepts which are most important are
Brahma, Maya, Transmigration of Souls, and Karma.
II. An essay of Emerson's, "The Over-Soul," contains many
ideas which are related to the Hindu Brahma.
III. Emerson's poem "Brahma" is similar to Hindu poems
found in the *Upanishads* and the *Bhagavad-Gita*.

Conclusion:
Ralph Waldo Emerson, in his poetry and essays, shows
the influence of Hindu philosophy and literature.

Errors

1. _____
2. _____
3. _____
4. _____
5. _____
6. _____
7. _____
8. _____
9. _____
10. _____

Application

Now you are ready to shape your material into an outline. Here is a good procedure to follow.

Objective: To prepare a sentence outline for your paper.

Procedure:

1. Work with your note cards until you have organized them in the best possible way.

2. Go through the ordered note cards, organizing the ideas in outline form, and expressing each idea in a complete sentence.

3. Check your note cards to be sure they are in the same order as your outline. Then number the note cards consecutively and write the number of each card in the appropriate place in your outline.

Step 12 — Writing Several Drafts

Application

Now that you have completed your outline, you are ready to write your research paper. You will probably have to rewrite the paper at least twice. You may find that some sections need many revisions to make them sound right. After each draft refer to the Self-Evaluation Guide in Appendix D for help in judging your own work critically.

Objective: To write as many drafts and revisions of your paper as are necessary to satisfy *you*. (Of course, the higher *your* standards are, the better your paper will be.)

Procedure:

1. The First Draft: The aim of the first draft is to turn your outline into smoothly flowing prose in which the sentences in the outline have been expanded, added to, and linked together. It may help you at this point to refer to the list of transitional words and phrases in Appendix C. When you use sentences from your outline which are followed by numbers (those that refer to note cards), be sure to transfer the numbers to your draft. As you work, concentrate on getting your ideas down with good style. Remember to refer to the Self-Evaluation Guide regularly.

2. The Second Draft: The aim of writing a second draft is to polish and perfect your paper. Reread your first draft critically. You can do this better if you wait a day or two between writing the first draft and rereading it. Revise all those sections which you can improve. Some parts of the paper may need several revisions; some may need none. Then check your spelling, grammar, punctuation, capitalization—in other words, concentrate on the form of your paper.

3. Additional Drafts: You may feel the need to do a third or even a fourth draft; keep reworking your paper until you are satisfied. When you think that you are ready to write a final draft, you should proceed to Step 13 so that you will be able to include the footnotes at the same time.

Step 13 — Footnoting; The Final Draft

In writing your paper you have depended upon facts, ideas, and opinions gathered in the course of your research. Every writer is under an obligation to point out the places where he depends upon the words or thinking of someone else and to cite the person whose work he is using. The single exception to this practice is material that is common knowledge. It is of course impossible to say exactly what constitutes common knowledge in a particular field. But certainly ideas and information that you have come across repeatedly in your research, and have found in several different sources, can be regarded as such. There will be many borderline cases. In the papers you write for your courses, it is perhaps the safest practice to footnote when in doubt.

A footnote reference consists of two parts, a marker in the text, usually a small raised number, and the footnote itself, identified with a corresponding number and usually placed at the bottom of the page. In the paper you are writing, you should place footnotes at the bottom of the appropriate page and number them consecutively throughout. When you are typing your paper, you will need to plan ahead in order to have room for the footnotes.

The proper footnoting of your paper began when you were doing your research and making out bibliography cards and note cards. The process continued as you carried the numbers of your note cards from your outline through the various drafts of your paper. When you are ready to do the final draft it is time to expand these numbers into footnotes.

This is done by using the number in the text to locate the original note card and using the reference on the note card to locate the relevant bibliography card. All the information you need to write a footnote will be found on these two cards, the description of the source on the bibliography card and the specific page number on the note card.

The form of a footnote is also important. Forms for three different kinds of sources are given in the Presentation below. Forms for other kinds of sources can be found in Appendix B. If you are going to be referring to the same source more than once in your paper, it will save you time to use short forms, which are also explained in Appendix B.

Presentation

Following are three footnotes. After each footnote you will find the bibliography card and the note card from which the footnote information was taken. The forms for these and other kinds of footnotes can be found in Appendix B.

1. Footnote entry for a book

[1] David Stevens, *Patterns of Population Growth* (Hartsdale, N.Y.: Sydney Mark, Inc., 1963), p. 39.

Stevens, David

Patterns of Population Growth

Hartsdale, N.Y.

Sydney Mark, Inc.

1963

future population

Stevens

39

The rate of population growth may decline in the future but the actual numbers of persons may increase.

example I U.S. population =
1980 rate of growth less
but actually more
people — 200 million +

2. Footnote entry for an article

² Bea Edelson, "Reconstructing Custer," *American History Quarterly*, 42 (Spring, 1969), pp. 153, 154.

Edelson, Bea

"Reconstructing Custer"

American History Quarterly

42

Spring, 1969

pgs. 150 - 163

soldiers'
number

Edelson   *153, 154*

I Numbers of active participants

in last battle

Indians = 1105

Custer = 136

3. Footnote entry for an anonymous article

[3] "Does Emerson Predict the American Hindu of the '70's?" *Cultural Exchange Journal*, 4 (Sept., 1973), p. 57.

Anonymous

"Does Emerson Predict the American

Hindu of the '70's?"

Cultural Exchange Journal

4

Sept., 1973

pgs. 56-58

Applying Emerson today

Does Emerson Predict   57
American Hindu of 70's

"The middle class American who has tried Yoga, Brahma, the Gita knows almost nothing of Emerson as a poet of the Orient as shown in a survey of 2/3 such subjects."

Recognition

Below are three footnotes which are written incorrectly. Rewrite them, using the forms in Appendix B. Concentrate on punctuation, indentation, and spacing. Then check the answer key in Appendix A.

[1] Leibman, Judith German Myth and History   Karlotto Press 1972   p. 81.   Branford, Conn.

[2] Sheila Peters   The New Role of Housewife   Readers' Magazine 6   March, 1969   pp. 70, 71

[3] Achievement Goals in Advertising   Buyers' Journal   30   Fall 1961   p. 95

Application

This Application should be done at the same time as the final draft of the paper.

Objective: To prepare footnotes for your paper that are correct in form and content.

Procedure:

1. As you do the final draft, turn the numbers in the text into footnotes, getting the necessary information from your note cards and bibliography cards and using the forms given in Appendix B. Number the footnotes consecutively throughout the paper.

2. Omit footnotes for any material that can fairly be called common knowledge.

3. Whenever possible use short forms as explained in Appendix B.

4. Type the footnotes at the bottom of the appropriate pages, separating them from the last line of the text by a double-space, a line about 1½ inches long (use the underscore key), and another double-space. Indent the first line of each footnote five spaces. Type footnote numbers slightly above the line.

Step 14 — Preparing the Bibliography

The bibliography is an alphabetical listing of all the sources you have used in writing your paper. It is fairly easy to prepare because most of the work was done during the research process when you made out your bibliography cards. In fact, the bibliography can be typed directly from the cards. The Presentation below gives the correct forms for three kinds of sources. Forms for other kinds of sources can be found in Appendix B.

Presentation

Below are three bibliography entries followed by the cards from which they were taken.

1. Bibliography entry for a book

Weinstein, Rosalie. *The History of the American Frontier.* New York: Russell and Russell, 1968.

Weinstein, Rosalie

The History of the American
Frontier

N.Y.

Russell and Russell

1968

2. Bibliography entry for an article

Gittelson, Ellen. "Modern Music's Symbols." *Music Digest*, 6 (Spring, 1970), 39–47.

Gittelson, Ellen

"Modern Music's Symbols"

Music Digest

6

Spring, 1970

pgs. 39 to 47

3. Bibliography entry for an anonymous article

"New York's Newest Union." *New York Today*, 4 (April 10, 1969), 41–50.

Anonymous

" New York's Newest Union "

New York Today

4

Ap. 10, 1969

pgs. 41 to 50

Recognition

Following are three bibliography entries which are written incorrectly. Rewrite these entries correctly using Appendix B. Concentrate on punctuation, indentation, and spacing. Check your answers with those given in Appendix A.

Debra Corbie   Hindu Myth and American Literature   New York Present Press Inc.   1970

Appleby, Jill   A Puerto Rican Pictorial History   Life   61 April 17, 1967   pgs. 27–32

Custer and Conformity   Historical Review LIII   Fall   1965 79–86

Application

The bibliography will be the last section of your paper. As with footnotes, it is important to give the information accurately and to maintain good form. The following procedure will help you do this.

Objective: To prepare a bibliography for your paper that is correct in form and content.

Procedure:

1. Take all your bibliography cards and arrange them in alphabetical order according to the author's last name, or where there is no author, the first word of the title (ignoring *a*, *an*, and *the*).

2. Type the entries directly from the cards, using the forms given in Appendix B. If an entry takes more than one line, the second and subsequent lines should be indented, usually five spaces. Be sure to match the commas, the underlining, and the spacing that are shown in Appendix B.

Step 15 — Creating a Title

Application

Now is the time to start thinking about a final title for your paper. Perhaps you have had a title in mind for some time. In that case the following procedure will give you a chance to consider other possibilities.

Objective: To create a title that will be suitable for your paper.

Procedure:

1. Think about your topic, your thesis, and the final draft of your paper. Then think of at least three titles that you could use. One might be explanatory, telling what is in the paper; another might be more fanciful,

trying to catch the spirit of what you have done. Don't give up too easily on this. You should spend at least fifteen minutes trying to get some fresh ideas.

2. Of the titles you have thought of, select the one that you feel will be most suitable for your paper.

Step 16 — Typing and Proofreading the Paper

Application

Once you have completed a final draft with footnotes in place, it is time to think of the final typing of the paper. The following procedure will give you some useful guidelines.

Objective: To produce a final paper that is accurate and attractive.

Procedure:

1. Use 8½-by-11-inch paper. Leave a margin of one inch at the top and bottom and of 1¼ inches at each side.

2. Double-space the entire paper with the following exceptions:

   (a) single-space within individual footnotes and bibliography entries, but double-space between footnotes and bibliography entries.

   (b) a long quotation should be single-spaced and given extra indention at both right and left. Here is an example:

It is necessary to develop a concept of the Hindu "Brahma." This element is basic to any study of Hindu philosophy and its application to morality is most interesting:

> "Brahma" in the ancient Hindu sense, refers to supreme all-pervading spirit of life. This spirit is the activating life force. It is eternal, non-divisible, non-destructible, non-creatable.[16]

Emerson took this concept, Yankee-fied it and brought it to popularity.

3. Indent the first line of each paragraph and footnote five spaces. Indent every line of a bibliography entry five spaces except the first.

4. Center page numbers at the top of the page or place them in the upper right-hand corner.

5. Place footnotes at the bottom of the appropriate pages. Between text and footnote, double-space, type a line about 1½ inches long, and double-space again.

6. Always make at least one copy of your paper, either a carbon or a machine copy, because sometimes papers are lost.

7. You are not going to be judged on your skill as a typist and the final copy need not be letter perfect. It should be carefully proofread, however, and any mistakes corrected neatly. Here are some commonly used proofreading marks which you may find helpful:

   ⁋ indicates that a new paragraph should begin.

   ∧ indicates where something is to be inserted.

   pᵃper   I ᵃᵐgoing home

   ∿ indicates that letters or words should be reversed

   research   New City York

   For other errors, cross out the mistake neatly with *one* line only and write the correct version in the space above the error.

8. Now is the time to give everything a last minute check. Do you have all the parts: cover page, text, bibliography, possibly illustrations or other supplementary material? When you have everything together in the right order, you can place it in a plastic see-through binder, which will protect your work and add to its appearance.

APPENDIX

A — ANSWERS TO EXERCISES

Step 2 — Recognition

1. I (technical)	6. B
2. G	7. G
3. G	8. I (personal)
4. I (narrow)	9. B
5. G	10. G

Step 3 — Recognition

1. e — the writer will give reasons why he thinks Bach is the greatest musician.
2. a — the writer will trace discrimination in the U.S. Army from 1900 through 1946.
3. d — the writer will discuss experts' solutions to the problems found in our welfare system.
4. c — the writer will analyze customs related to the topics religion, marriage, and birth.
5. b — the writer will compare Anthony and Roosevelt as they relate to his definition of a liberated woman.

Step 5 — Recognition

1. N — This is not a complete sentence.
2. T
3. T
4. N — This statement has no definite topic; we don't know which society or what aspects of the environment the writer will deal with.
5. T — Did you notice that statement 5 changes statement 4 into a good thesis statement?

6. N — This statement contains no definite topic or basic idea.

7. N — This statement does not rely on research since it is only a personal opinion.

8. T

9. T

10. T

Step 7 — Recognition

1. The most appropriate catalog card is (b), because it deals precisely with the topic and the thesis statement. The most appropriate index entry is (e), because it has the only article title which mentions unions specifically.

2. The most appropriate catalog card is (i), because its title shows the main topic of the book is migration *from* Puerto Rico. The most appropriate index entry is (l), since it deals with Puerto Ricans leaving the island and it was written during the decade mentioned in the topic and thesis.

Step 8 — Recognition

Errors on the bibliography card for a book

2 — author's last name is written first

3 — book title should be underlined

4 — the place of publication is missing

6 — the year the book was published is missing

7 — no pages are listed on a bibliography card for a book

Errors on the bibliography card for a periodical

8 — the title of the article should appear in quotes

10 — the volume number of the periodical is missing

11 — the date of the periodical is missing

Step 9 — Recognition

1. (a)   Subtopic in upper left-hand corner is missing.

    (b) Exact page where information is found is missing from upper right-hand corner.

2. (a) The author's name is missing from the top center of the card.

3. (a) Note has nothing to do with subtopic. Note does not include research information: "an interesting group" is not new or meaningful information.

    (b) Exact page where information is found is missing from upper right-hand corner.

Step 11 — Recognition

1. Heading is incomplete — no title.
2. No thesis statement is given.
3. No patterns of organization are given.
4. Introduction has no opening sentences; only a thesis statement is given.
5. Main Idea Sentence I should be developed into at least four paragraphs, one for each of the four concepts. Each paragraph should have a main idea, supporting details, and even subdetails.
6. No development of details for Main Idea Statement II.
7. No development of details for Main Idea Statement III.
8. Conclusion is only a restatement of the thesis with no summary or conclusions.
9. No numbers for the student's note cards are given.
10. The student who wrote this outline would find it almost useless when he wrote his paper. It is too skimpy and the ideas are not developed adequately. There is no evidence that he actually researched his material.

Step 13 — Recognition

[1] Judith Leibman, *German Myth and History* (Branford, Conn.: Karlotto Press, 1972), p. 81.

[2] Sheila Peters, "The New Role of Housewife," *Readers' Magazine*, 6 (March, 1969), pp. 70, 71.

[3] "Achievement Goals in Advertising," *Buyers' Journal*, 30 (Fall, 1961), p. 95.

Step 14 — Recognition

Corbie, Debra. *Hindu Myth and American Literature.* New York: Present Press Inc., 1970.

Appleby, Jill. "A Puerto Rican Pictorial History." *Life*, 61 (April 17, 1967), 27–32.

"Custer and Conformity." *Historical Review*, LIII (Fall, 1965), 79–86.

B — DOCUMENTATION

When you write a research paper you use facts, ideas, and opinions from many sources. Unless this information is common knowledge in the field about which you are writing, you should give credit to the author, regardless of whether you have used his words exactly (direct quote) or expressed his ideas in your own words (paraphrase). This citation of sources also makes it possible for the reader to investigate the matters you have written about for himself.

The system by which a writer acknowledges his indebtedness to others is called documentation. For a research paper, documentation takes two forms: (1) a bibliography in which you list alphabetically all the sources you have consulted, and (2) footnotes, which are specific acknowledgments attached to the appropriate parts of the text. Both bibliography and footnotes should be given in a standard form. This appendix on documentation is designed as a quick reference that you can consult whenever you need to know what the standard forms are.

FOOTNOTES — GENERAL RULES

1. The first line of each footnote is indented five spaces from the left-hand margin. The subsequent lines begin at the left-hand margin.

2. Each footnote should be single-spaced with a double-space between footnotes.

3. When you type footnotes, double-space after the last line of text, type a line about 1½ inches long (use the

underscore key), double-space again, and begin your footnotes.

Be sure you are consistent and use the same form throughout the paper.

FORMS FOR FOOTNOTES

A footnote contains the author's name, the title, publication information, and the exact pages on which you found the information you've used in your paper. This data appears in the following order:

For a Book
1. Author's first name, middle initial (if given), last name; then a comma; then
2. The title of the book, underlined; then
3. Parenthesis, place of publication; then a colon; then
4. The name of the publisher; then a comma; then
5. The year of publication; then close parenthesis; then a comma; then
6. The exact pages on which the information you used originally appeared; then a period.

For an Article
1. Author's first name, middle initial (if given), last name; then a comma; then
2. The title of the article in quotation marks, with a comma before the closing quotation marks; then
3. The name of the periodical in which the article appeared, underlined; then a comma; then
4. The date the periodical appeared; then a comma; then
5. All the pages on which the information you have used appeared; then a period.

In addition to these standard forms for a book and an article, there are special forms for different types of sources. The most common are shown below. Using these examples and the general rules, you should be able to write correct footnotes for any sources you use.

Anonymous Work

Book:

[1] *Indian Lands* (New York: Genn Publishing Co., 1913), pp. 16–17.

Article:

[2] "The U.F.T. and the Schools," *Life*, 44 (October 5, 1969), p. 44.

Anthology

[3] Steve S. David, "The Migrant Puerto Rican," in *Modern Population Movement*, ed. Mark Syd (Calif.: Ben Press, 1959), p. 472.

Editor of a collection

[4] Janet Allen, ed., *Selected Lyrics from the Age of Rock* (London: New Sounds Press, 1965), p. 35.

Encyclopedia and Dictionaries

[5] "Ralph Waldo Emerson," *Encyclopedia of Biography* (1925), V, 440.

Interview

[6] Dr. Lewis Burrows, Personal interview, Mt. Sinai Hospital, New York, N.Y., June 3, 1968.

Letter

[7] Anya Ben-Theo, Personal letter, March 13, 1970.

Lecture

[8] Denise Totah, Lecture: "Oriental Design in Emerson's Poetry," Columbia University, New York, N.Y., October 5, 1974.

Multiple Authors

Two or three authors:

[9] Mark Korn, Syd Stevens, and Ceil Kusin, *An Approach to the Brahmins*, 4th ed. (New York: Appleby and Sons, 1944), pp. 45–46.

More than three authors:

[10] Dr. Ben Lapkin, *et al.*, *Praise the Beatles* (London: Simon and Schuster, 1969), p. 108.

Newspaper

No article title or author:

[11] *New York Times*, June 3, 1935, Sec. 4, p. 10.

Article title and author:

[12] Maury Allen, "A Growing Union," *New York Post*, March 20, 1967, Sec. 2, p. 45.

Article title, no author:

[13] "The Puerto Rican Melting Pot," *Miami Post*, March 14, 1952, p. 5.

Pamphlet

Organization as author:

[14] University of the State of New York, State Education Department, *Collective Bargaining for the Paraprofessional* (Albany, 1968), pp. 28–29.

No author:

[15] *Indian Land Treaties* (Washington, D.C.: 1875), p. 15.

Unpublished Work

[16] Millicent Lapkin, "A Study of Female Puerto Rican Migration to New York City" (Unpublished thesis, Lehman College, 1968), p. 5.

SHORT FORMS

There are two short forms which you can use when you are citing a source for a second time. They are called consecutive and nonconsecutive citations. Suppose you have used a source in your paper and have written a footnote according to previous instructions. Then you find that you are using the same source immediately again, or consecutively. For this second citation you may use the Latin *Ibid.*, meaning "in the same place." Your first citation of the source and the use of *Ibid.* would look like this:

[1] Phyllis Cash, *Emerson, An American Puzzle* (New York: Simon and Schuster, 1965), p. 45.

[2] *Ibid.*

If you have used a different page of the same source, then the second footnote would look like this:

[2] *Ibid.*, p. 49.

Now suppose that you use this same source again, but this time after having used several other sources. Now you need the short form for a nonconsecutive citation. This consists of the author's last name, a comma, and the page of the citation. The nonconsecutive citation would look like this:

[9] Cash, p. 106.

If you have used two or more books by the same author, you must include the title of the source in the nonconsecutive citation:

[11] Cash, *American Poets*, p. 56.

If you use these short forms, you will never have to write a complete footnote for any source more than once.

BIBLIOGRAPHY — GENERAL RULES

1. Each bibliography entry begins at the left-hand margin. Each subsequent line is indented (usually five spaces).

2. Each entry should be single-spaced with a double-space between entries.

3. Bibliography entries are arranged alphabetically by the author's last name with an appropriate title such as "A Selected Bibliography." Sometimes an organization, government agency, or committee may be considered the author of an item. If there is no author, the entry is listed by the first word of the title, excluding the articles (*a, an, the*).

4. If you are listing two or more items by the same author, you may use a horizontal line about one inch long (use the hyphen key) instead of the author's name in all entries after the first. For example:

    Cash, Phyllis. *Emerson, An American Puzzle.* New York: Simon and Schuster, 1956.
    _____. *Hindu Influence in America.* New York: Simon and Schuster, 1967.

5. Bibliography entries are *not* numbered.

FORMS FOR BIBLIOGRAPHY ENTRIES

The bibliography entry contains the author's name, the title, and publication information in the following order:

For a Book

1. Author's last name; then a comma; the author's first name and initial (if given); then a period; then
2. The title of the book, underlined; then a period; then
3. The place of publication; then a colon; then
4. The name of the publisher; then a comma; then
5. The year of publication; then a period.

For an Article

1. Author's last name; then a comma; the author's first name and initial (if given); then a period; then
2. The title of the article in quotation marks, with a period before the closing quotation marks; then
3. The name of the periodical in which the article appeared, underlined; then a comma; then
4. The date the periodical appeared; then a comma; then
5. All the pages on which the article appeared; then a period.

As with footnotes, there are special forms for different types of sources. The examples below are the bibliographical entries for the same sources used in the footnote examples.

Anonymous Work
Book:
Indian Lands. New York: Genn Publishing Co., 1913.
Article:
"The U.F.T. and the Schools," *Life*, 44 (October 5, 1969), pp. 44–48.

Anthology
David, Steve S. "The Migrant Puerto Rican" in *Modern Population Movement.* Ed. Mark Syd. Calif.: Ben Press, 1959.

Editor of a collection
Allen, Janet, ed. *Selected Lyrics from the Age of Rock.* London: New Sounds Press, 1965.

Encyclopedia and Dictionaries

"Ralph Waldo Emerson." *Encyclopedia of Biography.* (1925), V, 439–441.

Interview

Burrows, Dr. Lewis. Personal interview on Puerto Rican workers in a New York City hospital. Mt. Sinai Hospital, New York, N.Y., June 3, 1968.

Letter

Ben-Theo, Anya. Personal letter. March 13, 1970.

Lecture

Totah, Denise. Lecture: "Oriental Design in Emerson's Poetry." Columbia University, New York, N.Y., October 5, 1974.

Multiple Authors

Two or three authors:

Korn, Mark, Syd Stevens, and Ceil Kusin. *An Approach to the Brahmins.* 4th ed. New York: Appleby and Sons, 1944.

More than three authors:

Lapkin, Dr. Ben, *et al. Praise the Beatles.* London: Simon and Schuster, 1969.

Newspaper

No article title or author:

New York Times, June 3, 1935, Sec. 4, p. 10.

Article title and author:

Allen, Maury. "A Growing Union," *New York Post.* March 20, 1967, Sec. 2, pp. 45–51.

Article title, no author:

"Puerto Rican Melting Pot, The," *Miami Post.* March 14, 1952, pp. 5, 8–10.

Pamphlet

Organization as author:

University of the State of New York, State Education Department. *Collective Bargaining for the Paraprofessional.* Albany: 1968.

No author:

Indian Land Treaties. Washington, D.C.: 1875.

Unpublished Work

Lapkin, Millicent. "A Study of Female Puerto Rican Migration to New York City." Unpublished thesis. Lehman College, 1968.

Salvatore L. Scorzello
ACS 110-8
April 10, 1975

THE CONDITION OF THE AMERICAN INDIAN

Professor Phyllis Cash

TABLE OF CONTENTS

The Condition of American Indians

<u>Charts</u>
Median Income of Indians, Non-
whites, and all Males (Selected
years, 1939-1964)

Median Family Income (Selected
Reservations, 1964)

Unemployment Rates: Indians,
Non-whites, and all Males (Selected years, 1940-1967)

Percentage Distribution of Years
of School Completed: Indians,
Blacks and all Males (1940, 1950,
1960)

Bibliography

The Condition of American Indians

Poverty in the United States of America is not uncommon nor is it partial to any race, creed, or color. However, when we look back into the history of America, we can find a case of severe destitution and want, concerning not just a group of people but a whole race - an Indian race of people who were rich in food, shelter and land at one time. A land which we call ours today is the United States of America, but in the truest sense of the word, it is "stolen property" for, in fact, the United States government took the land from the Indians and impoverished them.

It began with Christopher Columbus, who gave the people the name Indios. He described them as peace-loving, generous people. As it is quoted, he wrote to the King and Queen of Spain, "that I swear to your Majesties there is not in the world a better nation. They love their neighbors as themselves, and their discourse is ever sweet and gentle, and accompanied with a smile; and though it

-2-

is true that they are naked yet their manners are
decorous and praiseworthy." [1]

But, unfortunately, their ways were considered
a sign of weakness and the Europeans soon took ad-
vantage and undertook to enforce their ways upon
the people of the New World. The Europeans could
have learned something about their own relationship
to the earth from a people who were true conserva-
tionists.

Columbus kidnapped ten of his friendly Taino
Indians and carried them off to Spain, where they
could be introduced to the white man's ways. Span-
iards looted and burned villages and kidnapped hundreds of men, women and children so they could be
shipped to Europe and sold as slaves. The Taino and
Arawak tribes began to resist, thus bringing on the
use of guns and sabers, and whole tribes were destroyed - hundreds of thousands of people in less

---

[1] Dee Brown, <u>Bury My Heart At Wounded Knee</u> (New York:
Holt, Rinehart and Winston, 1970), p.1.

-3-

than a decade after Columbus set foot on the beach
of San Salvador, October 12, 1492. [2]

When the English-speaking white man arrived in
Virginia in 1607, they used subtler methods to in-
sure peace with the Powhatans who resided there. They
made a gold crown for Chief Wahunsona-cook and placed
it upon his head naming him King Powhatan and convinced him to put his people to work supplying the
white settlers with food. After Wahunsona-cook died,
the Powhatans rose up in revenge to drive the En-
glishmen back into the sea from which they had come,
but the Indians underestimated the power of English
weapons. In a short time, the eight thousand Powhatans were reduced to less than a thousand.[3] In each
state, they began somewhat differently but ended
virtually the same as in Virginia.

In Massachusetts and up and down the Pemaquid
land which we now call New England, the settlers
were coming by the thousands. So, in 1625, some

[2]Ibid., p.2.
[3] Ibid., p.3.

-4-

of the colonists asked Chief Samoset to give them
12,000 additional acres of Pemaquid land. Samoset
knew that the land came from the Great Spirit and
belonged to no man. Believing that the land was
as endless as the sky, he decided to humor these
strangers in their strange ways, and went through
a ceremony of transferring the land and made his
mark on a paper for them. It was the first deed of
Indian land to English colonists. [4]

Most of the other settlers did not bother to
go through such a ceremony. By the time Massasoit,
great Chief of the Wampanoags, died in 1662, his
people were pushed even further back into the wild-
erness. His son, Metacom, named King Philip by the
New Englanders, led his tribe and others in a war
against the white man in 1675 to save his and other
tribes from extinction. But, once again, the fire-
power of the colonists destroyed thousands of Indians and virtually exterminated the Wampanoag and

_____
[4] Ibid., p.3.

-5-

Naragansett tribes. King Philip was killed and his head publicly exhibited at Plymouth for twenty years. Along with other captured Indian women and children, his wife and young son were sold into slavery in the West Indies. [5]

For more than two centuries, these events were repeated again and again as the European colonists moved inland through the passes of the Alleghenies and down the westward flowing rivers to the Great Waters (the Mississippi) and then up the Great Muddy (the Missouri). [6]

The Five Nations of the Iroquois, mightiest and most advanced of all eastern tribes, strove in vain for peace. After years of bloodshed to save their political independence, they finally went down in defeat. Some escaped to Canada, some fled westward, some lived out their lives in reservation confinement. [7]

---

[5]Ibid., p.3.
[6]Ibid., p.4.
[7]Ibid., p.4.

-6-

During the 1760's, Pontiac of the Ottawas united tribes in the Great Lakes country in hopes of driving the British back across the Alleghenies, but he failed. [8]

A generation later, Tecumseh of the Shawnees formed a great confederacy of midwestern and southern tribes to protect their lands from invasion. The dream ended with Tecumseh's death in battle during the War of 1812. [9]

Finally, in 1829, Andrew Jackson, who was called Sharp Knife by the Indians took office as President of the United States. In his first message to the Congress, he recommended that all Indians be removed westward beyond the Mississippi. "I suggest the propriety of setting apart an ample district west of the Mississippi...to be guaranteed to the Indian tribes, as long as they shall occupy it." [10]

Although enactment of such a law would only add to the long list of broken promises made to the

[8] Ibid., p.4.
[9] Ibid., p.4.
[10] Ibid., p.5.

-7-

eastern Indians, Sharp Knife was convinced that Indians and whites could not live together in peace and that his plan would make possible a final promise which never would be broken again. On May 28, 1830, Sharp Knife's recommendations became law. [11]

Before these laws could be put into effect, a new wave of white settlers swept westward and the policy makers in Washington shifted the "permanent Indian frontier" from the Mississippi River to the 95th meridian. (This line ran from Lake of the Woods on what is now the Minnesota-Canada border). [12]

The decade following the establishment of the "permanent Indian frontier" was a bad time for the eastern tribes. The great Cherokee nation had survived more than a hundred years of the white man's wars, diseases and whiskey but when gold was discovered within their Appalachian territory, their removal to the West which was planned in gradual

---

[11] Ibid., p.5.
[12] Ibid., p.6

-8-

stages, became an immediate wholesale exodus. In
1838, General Winfield Scott's soldiers rounded them
up and concentrated them into camps. A few hundred
escaped to the Smoky Mountains and many years later,
were given a small reservation in North Carolina.
From the prison camps they were led westward to Indian Territory. On the long winter trek, one out of
every four Cherokees died from cold, hunger or disease. They called their march their "trail of
tears." [13]

Scarcely were the refugees settled in their so-
called "permanent Indian frontier" when the United
States went to war with Mexico. When the war ended
in 1847, the United States took possession of a vast
expanse of territory reaching from Texas to California. All of it was west of the "permanent Indian
frontier." [14]

Throughout the land, promises made by the white
man were broken, even after signing peace treaties

[13]Ibid., pp. 7-8.
[14]Ibid., p.8.

-9-

with the Indians. One particular example occurred
in the spring of 1868. The Great Warrior Sherman
(General Sherman) and Red Cloud (leader of the Sioux)
agreed to sign a peace treaty after a war that had
gone on for more than two years: "From this day for-
ward all war between the parties to this agreement
shall forever cease. The government of the United
States desires peace, and its honor is hereby pled-
ged to keep it. The Indians desire peace, and they
now pledge their honor to maintain it." [15]

For the next twenty years, however, the contents of the other sixteen articles of the treaty
of 1868 would remain a matter of dispute between the
Indians and the government of the United States.
What many of the chiefs understood was in the treaty
and what was actually written therein after Congress
ratified it, were like two horses whose colorations
did not match. (Spotted Tail, nine years later:
"These promises have not been kept....All the words

[15]Ibid., pp.140-141.

-10-

have proved to be false...There was a treaty made by
General Sherman, General Sanborn, and General Harney.
At that time the general told us we should have an-
nuities and goods from that treaty for thirty-five
years. He said this but yet he didn't tell the
truth." [16]

Consequently, our half million American Indians
are living today on reservations. An Indian reservation can be characterized as an open-air slum.
It has a feeling of emptiness and isolation. There
are miles and miles of dirt or gravel roads without
any signs of human life. The scattered Indian communities are made up of scores of tarpaper shacks
or log cabins with one tiny window and a stovepipe
sticking out of a roof that is weighted down with
pieces of metal and automobile tires. Each of these
dwellings, called homes, have as many as six or
seven people living in them. Some of the homes
have no electricity or running water - sometimes

[16]_Ibid_., pp. 141-142.

-11-

not even an out-house. The front yards are frequent-
ly littered with abandoned, broken-down automobiles
that are too expensive to repair and too much trouble to junk. [17]

The largest settlement on the reservation contains the officer of the Bureau of Indian Affairs
and the hospital, which is operated by the U.S. Public Health Service. The large modern homes of the
government employees stand in shocking contrast to
the shacks of the Indians. The stores in the town
are small but fairly modern. Very few Indians are
employed in them, and few are Indian-owned or man-
aged. [18]

The walls and shelves of the reservation trad-
ing post are lined with silver and turquoise articles as well as family treasures pawned by Indians
who will never save enough money to reclaim them.
Most of the items for sale have no price tags. What

_____

[17]Alan L. Sorkin, American Indians and Federal Aid
(Washington, D.C.: The Brookings Institution, 1971)
p.1.
  [18]Ibid., pp. 1-2.

-12-

better way to keep the Indian rug weavers or silver-
smiths who sell to the traders from learning the real
value of their work? The number of unemployed is
striking. Everywhere, there seems to be dozens of
Indians standing or sitting around doing nothing.
With so much time on their hands, many pass the day
drinking in bars just outside the reservation. [19]

Indians are, in general, stoic people. They
have learned to accept in silence the burdens of suf-
fering brought about by white domination. They wait
hours to see the Indian service doctor and to meet
with a Bureau of Indian Affairs official to discuss
payment of income from Indian lands leased to whites.
The Indians seldom complain about the wait or the
lack of chairs or the indifference with which they
are treated by the white officials. [20]

A survey taken in 1964 showed that the vast
majority of American Indians live in abject poverty;
74% of reservation families earned less than $3,000.

---

[19] Ibid., p.2.
[20] Ibid., p.2.

-13-

a year (the poverty threshold). While their income

rose considerably more between 1939 and 1964 than

that of the total population, it was only 30% of

the latter in 1964, as shown in the table on page

14. [21]

The table also shows a widening gap between

reservation and non-reservation Indians. In 1949,

the median income of the Indians on reservations

was 80% of the income of those living elsewhere; in

1959, the figure had dropped to 60%. The increased

disparity results from the migration of many rela-

tively well-educated and highly-skilled Indians to

major urban centers during the 1950's. In the met-

ropolitan areas, better paying jobs, more commesur-

ate with their level of ability, were available,

while the reservation economy remained comparatively

stagnant. [22]

---

[21]Ibid., p.8.
[22]Ibid., pp.8-9.

-14-

Median Income of Indians, Non-whites and all Males
Selected Years, 1939-1964
(In 1964 Dollars)
INDIANS

YEAR	ALL	NON-RESER-VATION	RESER-VATION	NON-WHITES	ALL MALES
1939	*n.a.	n.a.	500	925	2,300
1944	n.a.	n.a.	660	1,600	2,900
1949	950	1,040	825	1,925	3,475
1959	1,925	2,570	1,475	2,950	5,050
1964	n.a.	n.a.	1,800	3,426	6,283
Percent-age Increase, 1939-64			260	270	173

*n.a. - not available

As shown in the above table, from 1939 to 1964,
the median income of reservation Indians averaged
about half that of non-whites, which rose slightly
faster than that of reservation Indians during this
period. By 1959, the median income of non-reservation Indians was nearly that of non-whites. [23]

The source of income for reservation Indians

---

[23]Ibid., p.9

-15-

has changed fundamentally: in 1939, 38% came from

wages, 26% from agriculture, 8% from arts and crafts,

28% was unearned. In 1964, an estimated 75% of the

total income was derived from wages, with 10% from

agriculture, 5% from arts and crafts, and 10% was

unearned. [24]

There is great variation in income among reser-

vations. Median family income in 1964 varied from a

low of $900 on the Rosebud and Choctaw reservations

to $3,600. on the Northen Cheyenne reservation as

shown in the table on page 16. Even within the state

the variation is sizeable. In Montana, median income

on the Crow reservation was less than one-third of

that on the Northern Cheyenne reservation; in Ari-

zona, median income on the Papago and Hapi reserva-

tions was less than half that on the Salt River res-

ervation. [25]

There has been little change in the rank of the

states by individual Indian income; the states that

---

[24]Ibid., pp. 9-10.
[25]Ibid., p. 10.

-16-

were highest or lowest in 1950 generally were the
same in 1960. [26]

Median Family Income, Selected Reservations, 1964 [27]

Reservation	State	Median Family Income
Fort Apache	Arizona	$1,310.
Hopi	Arizona	1,140.
Papago	Arizona	900.
Salt River	Arizona	2,325.
Fort Hall	Idaho	2,235.
Leech Lake	Minnesota	2,039.
Choctaw	Mississippi	900.
Crow	Montana	1,100.
Northern Cheyenne	Montana	3,600.
Zuni	New Mexico	2,126.
Fort Berthold	North Dakota	1,544.
Turtle Mountain	North Dakota	2,228.
Pine Ridge	South Dakota	1,335.
Rosebud	South Dakota	900.

[26] Ibid., p.11.
[27] Ibid., pp. 12-13.

-17-

The strikingly low level of Indians income are

associated with unemployment rates several times

those of non-Indians (as shown in table on page 18).

While the rate for all males fell 64% between 1940

and 1960, the rate for all Indians rose 16%. The

increase is chiefly a result of the riot exodus of

Indians from agriculture in search of better paid

employment. Since most of them lack training and

education, they are restricted to unskilled occu-

pations with high rates of unemployment, particular-

ly on reservations where there has been little in-

dustrialization.

We must not forget that there were many pion-

eer organizers who, in good faith, sought to bring

about laws to secure land and protection for the

hapless Indians. Even though many of these laws

proved to be inadequate, the losses ultimately suf-

fered by the Indians could have been even greater.

However, there have been bills and laws passed

that, to this day, proved to be a long and bitter

-18-

Unemployment Rates: Indians,Non-whites,and all Males
     Selected Years, 1940-67 (in percent) [28]
                 INDIANS

YEAR	ALL	NON-RESER-VATION	RESER-VATION	NON-WHITES	ALL MALES
1940	32.9	*n.a.	n.a.	18.0	14.8
1950	n.a.	15.1	n.a.	9.6	5.9
1958	n.a.	n.a.	43.5	13.8	6.8
1959	n.a.	n.a.	48.2	11.5	5.3
1960	38.2	12.1	51.3	10.7	5.4
1961	n.a.	n.a.	49.5	12.8	6.4
1962	n.a.	n.a.	43.4	10.9	5.2
1965	n.a.	n.a.	41.9	7.4	4.0
1966	n.a.	n.a.	41.9	6.3	3.2
1967	n.a.	n.a.	37.3	6.0	3.1

*n.a. - not available

campaign for a complete overhaul of Indian affairs.
One such bill was the so-called Bursum Lands Bill
in 1922.

    This bill proposed to establish a procedure

[28] Ibid., pp. 12-13.

-19-

by which white settlers could perfect title to lands
which they had entered and improved or purchased in
good faith (so they claimed), believing the land to
be part of the public domain and open to homestead
entry, or held in private ownership and subject to
conveyance. In reality, the lands lay inside the
boundaries of grants conveyed by Spain to the Pueblo
Indians in New Mexico. The proposed legislation
placed upon the Indians the burden of proving their
lawful ownership, thus reversing the established
legal procedure which requires a person in adverse
possession to prove ownership. Some 3,000 white
squatters or families, representing perhaps 12,000
persons, and many thousands of acres were involved.[29]

The campaign of public education which brought
about the defeat of the original Bursum proposal
and the eventual passage of an equitable Pueblo
Lands Act also called forth new citizens groups,
two of which are still active in Indian Affairs.

[29]Robert C. Euler and Henry F. Dobyns, "Ethnic
Group Land Rights in the Modern State," Human
Organization, 3(1961-62), p.210.

-20-

The New Mexico Association, now the Southwestern Association on Indian Affairs, was formed in 1922 and
the American Indian Defense League followed soon
after. The latter organization experienced several
structural changes. One group moved its base of op-
erations eastward to become the Eastern Association
on Indian Affairs, and later changed its name to the
National Association on Indian Affairs, and still
later (1936) formed a new amalgamation with the par-
ent Indian Defense League. The resulting organization is the Association on American Indian Affairs of today - sometimes referred to in hostile
government reports as...that eastern organization
for Indians. [30]

Another law of inadequacy was the law of May
28, 1830. In connection with a series of treaties,
it set apart for the Indians the country lying west
of Missouri and Arkansas, and provided for the removal there of numerous tribes, not only from the
reservations east of the Mississippi, but also

[30] Ibid., p.210.

-21-

from the states and organized territories west of
that river. Between 1840 and 1850, the map showed
an "Indian Territory," stretching from the Red River
to the Platte, while the Sioux and other tribes re-
tained, almost unnoticed, the country further north.
In a few years, however, conditions demanded the organization of the northern portions of this great
tract. [31]

We must realize that the loss of land and economic status of the American Indian is closely related to his educational attainment. The median
level of schooling of the Indian male in 1960 was
about the same as the 1940 level of all males (as
shown in the table on page 22). Although the median
level of Indians increased by nearly three years
from 1940 to 1960, in 1960 the percentage of Indians attending college was only about one-third
that of all males, and the percentage of Indians
with no schooling or fewer than five years was more

[31]Roy Gittinger, "The Separation of Nebraska and
Kansas From the Indian Territory," Mississippi
Valley Historical Review, 3(March 1914-20)p.442.

-22-

than double that of all males. Between 1940 and 1960,

the median educational attainment of Indians and

Blacks was about the same, while two to three times

as many Indians as Blacks had no formal education.

Percentage Distribution: Years of School Completed [32]
   Indians, Blacks and all Males, 1940, 1950, 1960

Years of School Completed	Indians 1940, 1950, 1960			Blacks 1940, 1950, 1960			All Males 1940, 1950 1960		
0	23.4	14.7	9.6	8.0	7.4	5.0	1.2	2.6	2.4
1-4	19.6	15.1	12.6	32.8	28.7	17.7	5.4	9.3	7.0
5-8	37.8	38.3	37.8	40.5	37.2	36.2	41.7	37.2	32.4
9-11	9.4	15.4	22.8	9.7	11.5	22.7	19.8	16.3	18.7
12	4.8	7.7	11.6	4.5	6.8	12.1	18.2	17.6	21.2
13-15	2.0	2.3	4.0	1.8	2.6	4.0	6.9	6.8	9.8
16 or more	0.7	1.0	1.6	1.1	1.9	2.2	5.7	7.0	9.6
not reported	2.3	5.4	--	1.8	4.0	--	1.1	3.1	--
median	5.5	7.3	8.4	5.3	6.4	8.3	8.7	9.0	10.3

[32]Sorkin, p. 16-17.

-23-

Even up to this date, the Indian's pitiful plight has not ended. Just eight years ago, without notice to the Fort Mohave tribe of Indians or to the Bureau of Indian Affairs, the Solicitor's office conducted a proceeding initiated by California in the Bureau of Land Management whereby 1,500 acres of invaluable Indian land was awarded to California by a decision dated March 15, 1967, allegedly as coming within the Swamp and Overflow Act. Only by chance, when the matter was then on appeal, did it come to the Bureau of Indian Affairs to intervene. The Solicitor, it was said, perhaps facetiously but none the less officially, was representing the Bureau, although the Bureau was given no notice or opportunity to be heard. Under the most severe restrictions, the Indians were allowed drastically limited intervention. An astounding fact was forcefully brought to the Indians' attention: The Solicitors' position was not the Lawyer for the Trustee, the United States; rather, he emphasized, he was judge and, in fact, owed a trust obligation to California. Anomalous? Not

-24-

at all; that's the law as enunciated by the Solici-

tor. The matter is now before the Secretary of the

Interior for reconsideration. It is but a single

example of outrageous conduct by conflicting agen-

cies within the Interior Department, perpetrated

against the Mohaves in regard to their lands which

are inseparable from their rights to the use of

water. [33]

The early history of the United States and the

part the American Indian played reveals through ana-

lysis that the government took the land from the

American Indians and impoverished them.

The beginning of impoverishment started with the

first kidnapping of Indians into slavery, followed by

mass murder; destruction of villages and continuous

forceful movement of Indians. The Indians sought re-

venge but many died in vain. They trusted in the

white man's peace treaties with them but promises

---

[33] Joint Economic Committee Congress of the United
States, American Indian Fact and Future, (Washington:
United States Printing Office, 1969), pp. 514-515.

-25-

were continuously broken down through the years up to this present date.

A quotation by Heinmot Tooyalaket (Chief Joseph) of the Nez Perces, explicitly expresses how they feel about this land: "The earth was created by the assistance of the sun, and it should be left as it was...The country was made without lines of demarcation, and it is no man's business to divide it. ...I see the whites all over the country gaining wealth, and see their desire to give us lands which are worthless....The earth and myself are of one mind. The measure of the land and the measure of our bodies are the same. Say to us if you can say it, that you were sent by the Creative Power to talk to us. Perhaps you think the Creator sent you here to dispose of us as you see fit. If I thought you were sent by the Creator I might be induced to think you had a right to dispose of me. Do not misunderstand me, but understand me fully with reference to my affection for the land. I never said the land was mine to do with it as I chose. The one who has the right to

-26-

dispose of it is the one who has created it. I claim

a right to live on my land, and accord you the privi-

lege to live on yours." [34]

---

[34]Brown, p.300.

-27-

BIBLIOGRAPHY

Brown, Dee. <u>Bury My Heart At Wounded Knee</u>. New York: Holt, Rinehart and Winston, 1970.

Euler, Robert C. and Henry F. Dobyns. "Ethnic Group Land Rights In The Modern State." <u>Human Organization</u>. 3 (1961-62) p. 210.

Gittinger, Roy. "The Separation of Nebraska and Kansas From The Indian Territory." <u>Mississippi Valley Historical Review</u>. 3 (March 1914-20) p. 442.

Joint Economic Committee Congress of the United States. <u>American Indian Fact and Future</u>. Washington: United States Printing Office, 1969.

Sorkin, Alan L. <u>American Indians and Federal Aid</u>. Washington, D.C.: The Brookings Institution, 1971.

C — TRANSITIONAL WORDS AND PHRASES

1. *Addition*: one, another, similarly, moreover, furthermore, in addition, too, again, equally important, next, finally, first, second (etc.), besides, likewise, in the same way.

2. *Contrast*: yet, however, still, nevertheless, on the one hand/on the other hand, on the contrary, notwithstanding, for all that, by contrast, at the same time, although, while, a different view, in spite of, despite,

3. *Comparison*: similarly, likewise, in like manner, both, each, in the same way.

4. *Conclusion*: therefore, thus, then, consequently, as a consequence, as a result, accordingly, finally, for this (these) reason(s), on that account, because of, under these conditions, since.

5. *Explanation*: for example, to illustrate, by way of illustration, to be specific, specifically, in particular, thus, for instance, in other words.

6. *Concession*: naturally, granted, of course, to be sure, although, despite, in spite of, notwithstanding, for all, while.

7. *Time*: when, immediately, upon, since, first, earlier, meanwhile, at the same time, in the meantime, soon afterward, subsequently, later.

8. *Summation, Repetition, Intensification*: to sum up, in brief, in short, in fact, indeed, in other words.

D — SELF-EVALUATION GUIDE

Form
1. Will your paper be ready on time? Many instructors lower the grades on late papers.
2. Is your paper the correct length? Most students write papers which are too short rather than too long.

3. Footnotes — a) Do they follow the correct form?
   b) Are they placed properly?

4. Bibliography — a) Have you used enough sources?
   b) Have you followed the correct form?

5. Is your paper neatly typed with few errors and proper margins?

6. Have you met *all* the specifications given by this book or your instructor?

Style

1. Is your paper well-organized? Does each part relate to the whole? Does the development of your ideas follow a logical order?

2. Is your grammar, spelling, and punctuation correct?

3. Does your paper flow smoothly? Have you used transitional words and sentences to link the different parts of the paper?

4. Have you used synonyms to avoid too much repetition in your vocabulary?

5. Are your sentences clearly constructed—not too short or choppy; not too long or hard to follow?

Content

1. Are your topic and thesis relevant to the assignment you were given? Is your thesis important enough to write about?

2. Does your introduction really "introduce" your paper? Do you have a good opening sentence? Do you state your thesis so that the reader knows what your paper is about?

3. Does each succeeding paragraph amplify at least one main idea?

4. Have you used recognized, up-to-date sources? Have you used enough sources to substantiate your thesis? Have you used a variety of sources—books, periodicals, newspapers, interviews, etc.?

5. Does your conclusion summarize and restate your thesis in a final way, using the results of your research?

Final Evaluation

Can you grade your own paper in each of the above areas?

Form
Style
Content

A — excellent, outstanding work
B — very good
C — fair
D — poor
F — does not meet acceptable standards

NOTES

NOTES

NOTES

NOTES